W9-BXB-920

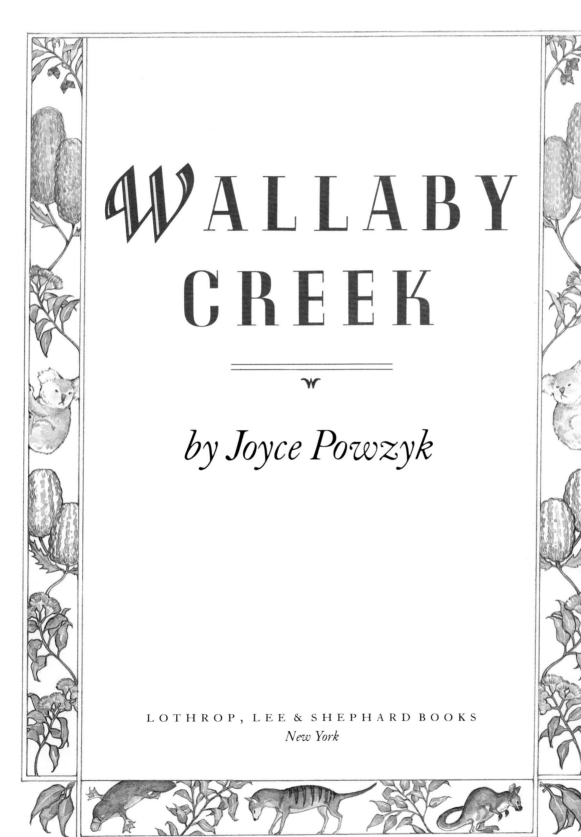

WALLABY CREEK

by Joyce Powzyk

LOTHROP, LEE & SHEPHARD BOOKS
New York

Acknowledgements

I would like to thank Kate Fitzherbert and David Baker-gabb of Victoria, Australia and Gerry Van Asch of Havelock North, New Zealand for their support and encouragement. Barbara McGuire provided me with valuable criticisms of the manuscript and my editor, Barbara Lalicki, was always close by, providing me with guidance and enthusiasm. I am also greatly indebted to Walter Boles, David McAlpine, and Debbie Kent of the Australian Museum in Sydney, Australia for allowing me to work from their vast collection of specimens. Mary LeCroy of the American Museum of Natural History in New York City was invaluable in securing Australian animal skins for study in completion of the book's illustrations. But to the Hayes families of Wallaby Creek, I must extend my deepest appreciation for taking me into their homes and extending their warm hospitality. The words and descriptions used in this book make use of the popular terminology I encountered while traveling and studying in Australia.   —J.P.

Sharp-eyed readers may be interested to know that, unlike the female, the male yellow-tailed black cockatoo has red eye-markings.

First Edition 1 2 3 4 5 6 7 8 9 10

Library of Congress Cataloging in Publication Data
Powzyk, Joyce Ann.   Wallaby Creek
Summary: The author describes the unique and varied
assortment of animals she observed during a stay at
Wallaby Creek, Australia. Her own watercolor paintings of goannas,
cockatoos, kookaburras, platypuses, wallabies, kangaroos,
koalas, dingoes, and other animals accompany her descriptions.
1. Wildlife watching—Australia—Wallaby Creek
(N.S.W.)—Juvenile literature.   2. Zoology—Australia—
Wallaby Creek (N.S.W.)—Juvenile literature.
3. Wallaby Creek (N.S.W.)—Juvenile literature.
[1. Zoology—Australia—Wallaby Creek (N.S.W.)
2. Australia.   3. Wallaby Creek (N.S.W.)   4. Wildlife watching]
I. Title.   QL339.N44P69   1985   599.09944
84-29757   ISBN 0-688-05692-X   ISBN 0-688-05693-8 (lib. bdg.)
Typography by Kathleen Westray

This book is dedicated to
I R I S & J A C K H A Y E S *and*
N E D & M A R G R E T H A Y E S *of*
Wallaby Creek, Australia

A N D M Y F A M I L Y

Over 55 million years ago, Australia was connected to a larger land mass that included today's Africa, South America, and the Antarctic. This supercontinent gradually broke apart, and Australia drifted off to become an island. The creatures that were stranded on Australia were an odd assortment, and, due to their early isolation, they evolved independently from the rest of the world. There was a rich diversity of birds, reptiles, and three different types of mammals: the monotremes, the marsupials, and the placentals. Those that dominated the land fell into the marsupial category, ranging from the large grazing kangaroos to the small possums of the forest. Today, these unique creatures continue to enhance the island continent and add to the fascination of the Land of Down Under.

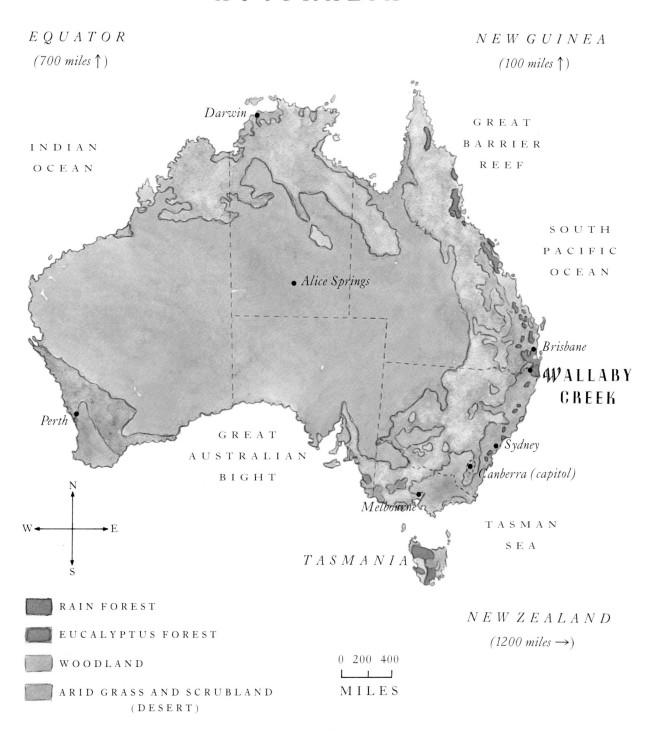

AUSTRALIA

EQUATOR
(700 miles ↑)

NEW GUINEA
(100 miles ↑)

Darwin •

INDIAN
OCEAN

GREAT
BARRIER
REEF

SOUTH
PACIFIC
OCEAN

• *Alice Springs*

• *Brisbane*

𝔚𝔞𝔩𝔩𝔞𝔟𝔶
ℭ𝔯𝔢𝔢𝔨

Perth •

GREAT
AUSTRALIAN
BIGHT

• *Sydney*

• *Canberra (capitol)*

Melbourne

TASMAN
SEA

N

W ← → E

S

TASMANIA

NEW ZEALAND
(1200 miles →)

RAIN FOREST

EUCALYPTUS FOREST

WOODLAND

ARID GRASS AND SCRUBLAND
(DESERT)

0 200 400

MILES

On the eastern seaboard of Australia, about a hundred miles from the Pacific Ocean, is a place called Wallaby Creek. In the spring of 1983, I spent several weeks there studying the native animals. Home was a small ranger's hut that stood on the edge of an open woodland area, shadowed by several towering old eucalyptus or gum trees.

The first night of my stay introduced me to the strange sounds of the Australian outback. These screeches and grunts lured me out into the bush, and I began to take long walks at any time of day or night.

Kangaroos and wallabies roamed freely through the fields of grass,
along with prowling monitor lizards. Nearby flowed the cool waters
of Wallaby Creek, for which the area is named. Beyond the creek
stood the dark and tangled rain forest, home to flying possums and
black cockatoos. Each animal possessed a distinctive behavior and moved
through the varied landscape, taking what it needed to live. In time,
I began to feel and understand the rhythm of life at Wallaby Creek.

It was March, the last month of Australia's long, hot summer. I spent the morning exploring a stream bed, stepping easily from one stone to the other because the water level was low. I reached down to have a drink and was startled by a beautiful eastern water dragon. With a full crest of sharp spines running down the center of its back, the lizard resembled a miniature dragon from an enchanted fairy tale. This creature was relying on its markings for camouflage as it lay motionless, just a few inches from my hand. As I continued to stare, afraid to move and break the spell, the lizard suddenly bolted, practically running across the water's surface before diving under for cover.

The eastern water dragon always makes its home near running water, a habitat that provides both food and security. Frogs, mice, insects, and even berries are food for the water dragon. One lizard that I disturbed dove from its hiding place high in the tree branches to the safety of the water below. This is an efficient escape for an animal that can remain underwater for up to thirty minutes.

Lesueur's frog

Physignathus leseurii   *Eastern Water Dragon*

The monitor lizard slowly skidded headfirst down the trunk of the bloodwood tree. The bark was badly scraped where its sharp claws had held tight to slow the fall. I stood nearby and noticed how its scaly skin was patterned with bands of yellow and black. As the lizard hit the ground, it spied me and fled into the bush. It was a lace monitor, named for its markings—and, being a young lizard, it was still shy.

When a member of this species is full-grown, it reaches a length of 6 feet and can become very aggressive, using its thick tail as a weapon. After frightening one such lizard, I decided to watch these reptiles from the hut's window. This proved to be the best way to follow their movements without causing alarm.

Many times I watched the monitor lizard, or goanna (go-an-na) as it is commonly called, search for food the same way a snake does, by tracking its prey with a forked tongue that is sensitive to body heat. When the goanna grabs its prey, it uses its powerful jaws and special teeth that point backward like shark teeth to hold and swallow food. The lace monitor will feast on whatever it can find, but favorite foods include rats, mice, birds, and any kind of dead meat or carrion.

Varanus varius

Lace Monitor

Calyptorhynchus
funereus

The majestic black cockatoo visited the creek on days that were exceptionally hot and dry. A small family group of three appeared in the late afternoon, flying down through the green curtain of rain forest. Hoarse, echoing screams announced their arrival. When one bird flew down to drink at the creek's edge, the others kept guard from their perches above. After satisfying their thirst, they moved to some neighboring trees and began to feed on pine seeds and wood-boring insects. One of the cockatoos used its strong, hooked bill to strip away the tree's outer bark and feed on the grubs living beneath.

Yellow-tailed Black
Cockatoo

The two adult birds were mates for life and had raised their single fledgling in a secluded nest high up in a tree hollow. This group was made up of yellow-tailed black cockatoos that were jet black except for a small yellow ear patch and some light yellow on their tail feathers.

The cockatoos eventually departed and flew back into the deeper haunts of the forest. Because they had three-foot wingspans, I was surprised by how easily they maneuvered through the tangle of leaves and vines. Each wingbeat was slow and deliberate, causing the birds to appear suspended as they flew through the air.

The laughing kookaburra was my constant companion during the daylight hours at Wallaby Creek. There were several of these birds scattered throughout the woodlands, defending their territories through song. I once heard an old Australian legend that if a person imitated the bird's laugh, the sky people who controlled the great sun would become angry and cause the earth to dwell in total darkness.

The kookaburra hunts by sitting motionless for hours on a tree limb, spying for movement in the tall grass below. After locating a possible meal, the bird suddenly plunges headlong, straight toward the ground. A dull thud is heard as the kookaburra strikes the prey with its body and sharp beak. The prey animal could be an insect, a lizard, or a small snake. The kookaburra then swallows its catch whole or carries it away to a safe feeding perch.

Before sunset, a kookaburra flew over the hut, its wings whistling softly before the bird landed in a nearby tree. It sang out its "*koo-hoo-ha-ha-ha*" call, quietly at first and then quickening and growing louder. From across the field, another kookaburra started up with its own cackling laughter. The cool air was filled with these eerie calls as dusk settled into night.

Dacelo gigas   *Laughing Kookaburra*

*Female satin
bowerbird*

During the Australian spring, the male satin bowerbird puts
together a beautiful arrangement of sticks called a bower. He carefully pokes twigs into the ground, forming them into a large U-shaped
structure with saliva and mud. I discovered one bower that contained
a yellow crest feather and five royal blue clothespins, probably stolen
from a nearby farm. The male bird collects these objects and
constantly rearranges them in the hope of attracting a mate. When a
female accepts a male, she crouches in the bower, and the wild
courtship begins. The excited male struts about, puffing up his
feathers while singing an unusual song composed of wheezes and
hisses. After mating, the female is quickly chased away by the male,
and she then chooses a site to build a nest. Here she will lay eggs and
hatch and raise the fledglings alone. The male bird's primary concern
in life is to attract more females to his elaborate construction of sticks.

While sketching in my hut, I was startled by a male satin bowerbird that boldly alighted in the doorway. He flashed his lilac-colored
eyes while carefully looking over my belongings for a new ornament.
Blue objects fascinate this species, and so I offered my blue drawing
pencil, but he turned it down and flew away. Perhaps he was searching
for a juicy insect, some ripened grapes, or another blue clothespin.

Ptilonorhynchus violaceus   Satin Bowerbird

*L*ate one night, loud gurgling noises were coming from the direction of the creek, and so I grabbed my flashlight and stole down to investigate. I sat quietly in the thick weeds, breathing in the strong aroma of eucalyptus while fighting off the biting ants. Many animals come to drink under the protection of night, and I thought this might be my chance to see a rare nocturnal wallaby. Then, to my surprise, a small webbed foot waved above the water's surface. The animal frolicked and somersaulted in the pool of water with its eyes closed. It was a little platypus, only 14 inches in length. The animal seemed to be playing as it scoured the creek's bottom for tasty worms and insect larvae, sifting through the mud and water with its sensitive, ducklike bill.

The Australian platypus belongs to a small, primitive order of mammals called Monotremata. This order is an important evolutionary link between two different classes of animal life, the reptiles and the mammals. The female platypus lays a leathery egg, similar to that of a reptile, which hatches after a two-week incubation. The baby is then nourished like a mammal, on milk that is secreted from the mother's underbelly.

I felt fortunate to have seen this rare and elusive creature in its wild habitat. The platypus continues to exist at Wallaby Creek because the local people have always worked hard to protect the land and its creatures.

Ornithorhynchus anatinus   *Platypus*

*Petaurus
breviceps*

While out on a twilight walk, I saw the excitable sugar gliders, moving through the upper tree branches as they chattered along the way. These noises are often used to warn fellow gliders that a dangerous owl or snake is lurking nearby. These small possums are quick, and even with the help of my flashlight, all that I could see was the movement of rustling leaves and the reflection of light in their little, beady eyes.

The sugar glider has a special adaptation for gliding, a large flap of skin that runs along each side of the body. This is stretched out as it jumps from its lofty perch to a neighboring tree trunk, sometimes gliding over 140 feet in distance before landing. The possum uses its tail as a rudder and lands on the tree trunk nose up, grabbing tightly with its claws before scampering up into the leaf canopy for cover.

*Sugar
Glider*

Although the glider's body is only 7 inches long, it is an aggressive
hunter, chasing moths and other insects throughout the forest. It also
enjoys feasting on sugary flower nectar and tree sap. The glider cuts a
V-shaped groove into the tree bark with its sharp incisor teeth and
licks up the oozing sap.

   At first glance, this animal resembles a small squirrel, but because
it is a marsupial, it has a different way of bearing its young. Marsupials are unique in that their babies are born underdeveloped and
completely blind. Guided by instinct, the infant crawls several inches
to find its way into the mother's protective stomach pouch. Here, the
infant is safe and will nurse on its mother's milk until weaned.

w

Eucalyptus blossoms

The brushtail possum ambled along the tree limb, its nose wet from sniffing through the rain-soaked leaves. This hungry animal was hoping to uncover a nest of robin's eggs or a clump of sweet eucalyptus blossoms. I could just make out its face and plump body as I peered up through the branches from the ground below. The brushtail is named for its fluffy tail, which has a naked area at the tip so the tail can grasp branches. A clawless thumb on each hind foot also helps the animal to find secure footing, while all the other toes have sharp claws as defense against owls or wild dingo dogs. Compared to its energetic cousin, the sugar glider, a brushtail moves much more slowly and can weigh up to 25 pounds!

I continued to walk through the rain forest and encountered a smaller brushtail possum on the ground. It immediately climbed the nearest tree and uttered a low, throaty *"kerrrr"* sound in warning. The Australian species of possums do not "play dead" to fool intruders like the North American opossums. I eventually went back to the hut and fixed a nice hot meal for supper. The aroma attracted the brushtails, which are never shy when it comes to raiding campsites or garbage cans for food. Even after I had settled down to sleep, the possums awakened me with their scratching at the door and loud footsteps across the hut's tin roof, as they tried to get in for a midnight snack.

Trichosurus vulpecula   *Brushtail Possum*

The red-necked wallaby bounded down the path towards the creek, making a dull thumping noise with each hop. I could easily recognize this species by the beautiful rusty red fur that covers its neck and shoulders. This was a female, heavy with a young wallaby, or joey, in her stomach pouch. After stopping for a drink, she started to groom herself by roughing up her fur and licking it back into place. The joey kicked its way free from her warm pocket and took a hop, high into the air with the help of its oversized hind legs. The joey's wiry little body bounced like a pogo stick around its mother, who gently reached out with her paw to settle the excited youngster.

I always found this species alone or in small, loose groups, ready to flee at the slightest hint of danger. The wallaby is very shy compared to the more gregarious gray kangaroo, which forms tight groups, or mobs, for protection. The main difference between a wallaby and a kangaroo is size. The red-necked wallaby has a smaller hind foot and is shorter in build, standing only 3 feet tall.

During the early evening hours, the wallabies grazed through the tall grass, their heads popping up occasionally to scan the countryside. One animal pulled down a tall flowering plant with its delicate hand-like paws and quietly stuffed its mouth full of petals. From somewhere out in the bush came loud grunting noises as two wallabies quarreled over a choice bit of grass.

Joey

Macropus rufogriseus   *Red-necked Wallaby*

A mob of eastern gray kangaroos dozed lazily under a stand of red gum trees. The noonday sun was hot, and the fields were alive with the heavy drone of insects. The adults were reclining on their sides, with their long hind legs outstretched. I closely watched their faces and noticed how their features looked remarkably like a cross between those of a deer and a llama. The animal's ears were large and full, twitching to every sound. The nose was slightly tapered and the eyes were impressive, a deep liquid brown color, heavily fringed with eyelashes. Despite the heat, two young males, or bucks, started acting frisky and became engaged in a mock boxing match. They jabbed each other with their forepaws, rocking back on their tails and throwing back their heads to absorb the punches.

The kangaroo belongs to a group of animals called macropods. All macropods have large hind feet which move in unison. When hurrying a 'roo can travel at speeds over 25 miles per hours, with jumps measuring 27 feet in length. The largest marsupial at the creek is the male gray kangaroo, which stands 5½ feet in height; while the female, or doe, stands 4 feet tall.

The kangaroos that I had been watching became wary of my presence and arose from their afternoon nap. They moved off across the meadow, hopping effortlessly, with their long tails bobbing behind them.

Macropus giganteus   *Eastern Gray Kangaroo*

---

w

𝒯he koala sat high up in the top of the eucalyptus tree, its body wedged precariously between the branches. Looking like a ball of gray fur, it slept away the daylight hours. Since the koala spends so much time sitting, its rump is padded with an extra layer of fat and dense fur for comfort. Another adaptation for tree life is a special viselike grip between the first two fingers and the last three, which allows the animal to hold on to the smooth bark of the eucalyptus tree.

At night, the koala is busy eating up to 2½ pounds of eucalyptus leaves. It gets all of its water from these leaves. Hence, the aborigines called this animal *koala*, which is an aboriginal word for "no drink." The female carries her baby in an unusual stomach pouch that opens at the bottom rather than the top. The little koala fits in tightly and cannot fall out. When the youngster gets older, it will ride on the mother's back like possums and other tree-climbing marsupials.

Although Wallaby Creek does not have many koalas, their loud, wailing cries can sometimes be heard at night, drifting across the hills. I spotted a mother and cub late one evening, traveling along the ground, probably in search of better feeding areas. The koala only eats the leaves of a few species of eucalyptus trees and must find new trees when the food supply becomes low.

Forefoot   *Hindfoot*

Phascolarctos cinereus   *Koala*

Scarab beetle

W

I sat in the brush, hidden from view, looking out over the land of Wallaby Creek. Every day had brought something new, whether it was a beetle, a kangaroo, or a brightly colored parrot. Just then, from across the field, came a wild dingo, walking quietly without so much as cracking a twig. The dingo was a soft blond color, and its body was slim but well-muscled for the hunt. Legend has it that only a full-blooded dingo has a white tip at the end of its tail, and indeed this creature had one. The dog's ears stood erect, and its nose was testing the air, but I was safely concealed downwind.

About 8,000 years ago, the first dingo arrived with the aborigines, having traveled through southern Asia into Australia. The dog was probably used as a hunting companion to help in chasing and cornering prey. It does not bark, but it howls or makes a yapping noise. For food this canine eats anything it can catch, including mice, possums, and wallabies. The dingo is not a marsupial but a placental mammal, giving birth and caring for its pups in the same manner as wolves or dogs.

Continuing its search for some unsuspecting prey, the dingo disappeared as silently as it had arrived. I remained in my hiding place and thought how important each animal was to the whole structure of life here at the creek. There are many other specialized ecosystems throughout the world that need similar respect and preservation. Wallaby Creek had brought me closer to one group of animals, and my experience there showed me how easily we can coexist.

Canis familiaris

Dingo